BEAUTIFUL ARCHITECTURE

COLORING BOOK OF BUILDINGS STRUCTURES

COLORING FOR 9 YEAR OLD

EDUCANDO KIDS

Enjoy coloring these beautiful architectural works of art!

ARCHITECTURAL WORKS

Coloring Pages

This is a Bleed Through Page If You Are Using a Coloring Marker or Pen!

Find Other Great Titles By searching for Educando Kids on Your Favorite Book Retailer

Amazon.Com | Barnes & Noble (BN.Com) | Books A Million (BAM.Com)

EDUCANDO KIDS

This is a Bleed Through Page If You Are Using a Coloring Marker or Pen!

Find Other Great Titles By searching for Educando Kids on Your Favorite Book Retailer

Amazon.Com | Barnes & Noble (BN.Com) | Books A Million (BAM.Com)

EDUCANDO KIDS

This is a Bleed Through Page If You Are Using a Coloring Marker or Pen!

Find Other Great Titles By searching for Educando Kids on Your Favorite Book Retailer

Amazon.Com | Barnes & Noble (BN.Com) | Books A Million (BAM.Com)

EDUCANDO KIDS

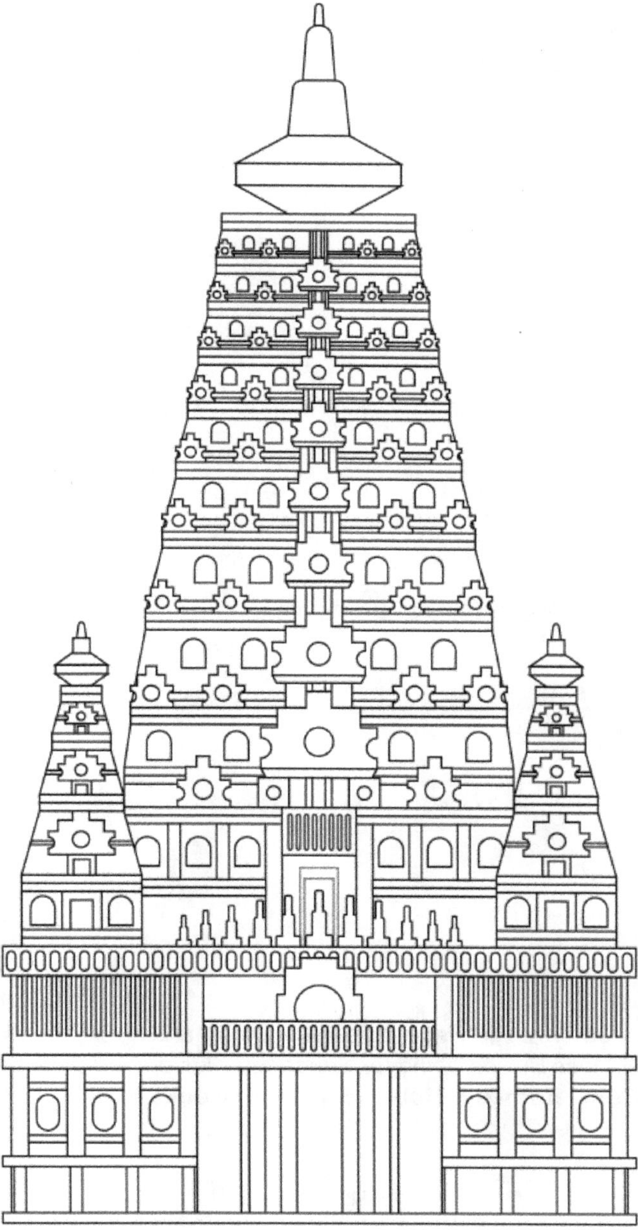

This is a Bleed Through Page If You Are Using a Coloring Marker or Pen!

Find Other Great Titles By searching for Educando Kids on Your Favorite Book Retailer

Amazon.Com | Barnes & Noble (BN.Com) | Books A Million (BAM.Com)

EDUCANDO KIDS

This is a Bleed Through Page If You Are Using a Coloring Marker or Pen!
Find Other Great Titles By searching for Educando Kids on Your Favorite Book Retailer
Amazon.Com | Barnes & Noble (BN.Com) | Books A Million (BAM.Com)

EDUCANDO
KIDS

This is a Bleed Through Page If You Are Using a Coloring Marker or Pen!

Find Other Great Titles By searching for Educando Kids on Your Favorite Book Retailer

Amazon.Com | Barnes & Noble (BN.Com) | Books A Million (BAM.Com)

EDUCANDO KIDS

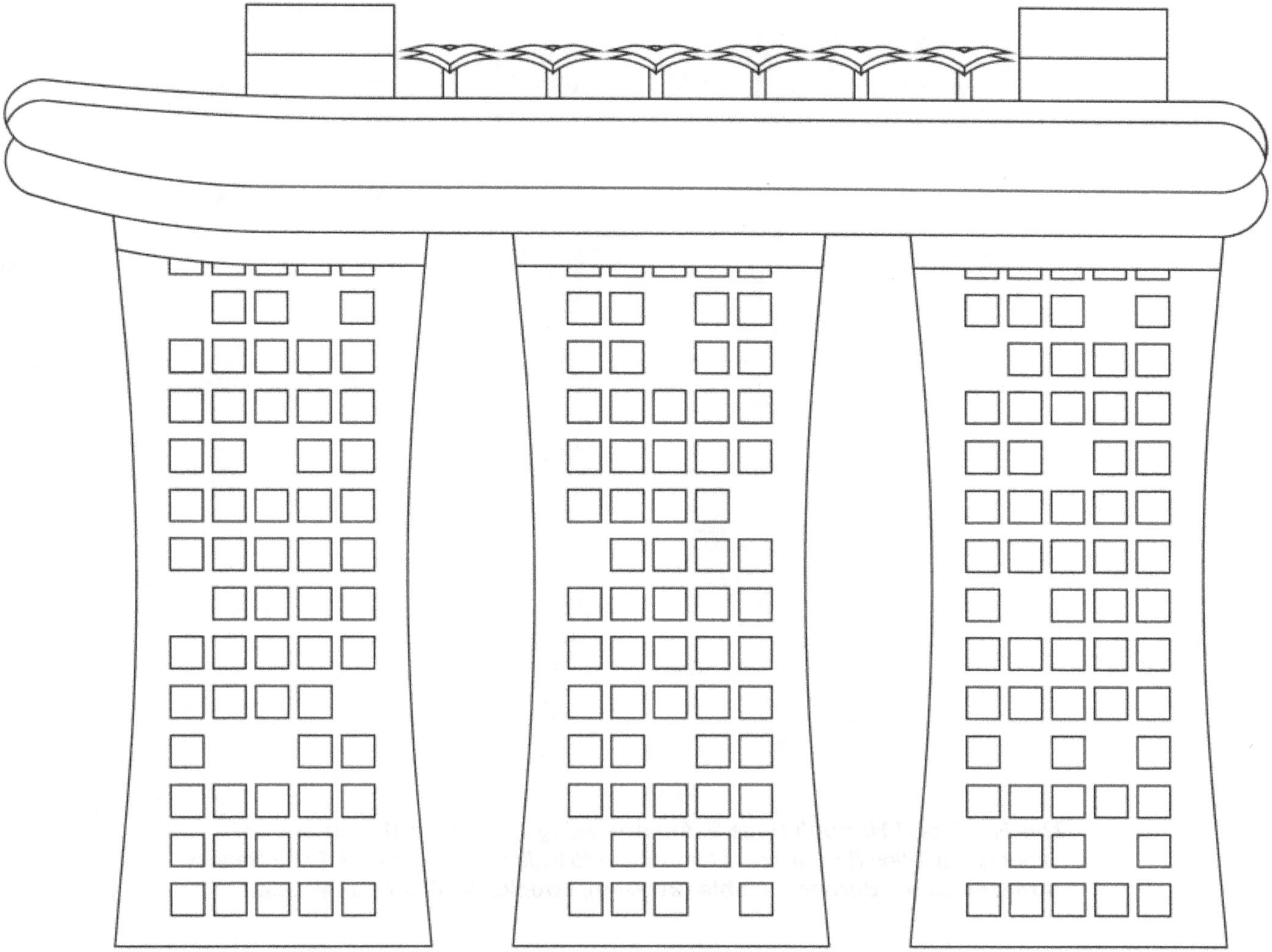

This is a Bleed Through Page If You Are Using a Coloring Marker or Pen!

Find Other Great Titles By searching for Educando Kids on Your Favorite Book Retailer

Amazon.Com | Barnes & Noble (BN.Com) | Books A Million (BAM.Com)

EDUCANDO KIDS

This is a Bleed Through Page If You Are Using a Coloring Marker or Pen!

Find Other Great Titles By searching for Educando Kids on Your Favorite Book Retailer

Amazon.Com | Barnes & Noble (BN.Com) | Books A Million (BAM.Com)

EDUCANDO KIDS

This is a Bleed Through Page If You Are Using a Coloring Marker or Pen!

Find Other Great Titles By searching for Educando Kids on Your Favorite Book Retailer

Amazon.Com | Barnes & Noble (BN.Com) | Books A Million (BAM.Com)

EDUCANDO KIDS

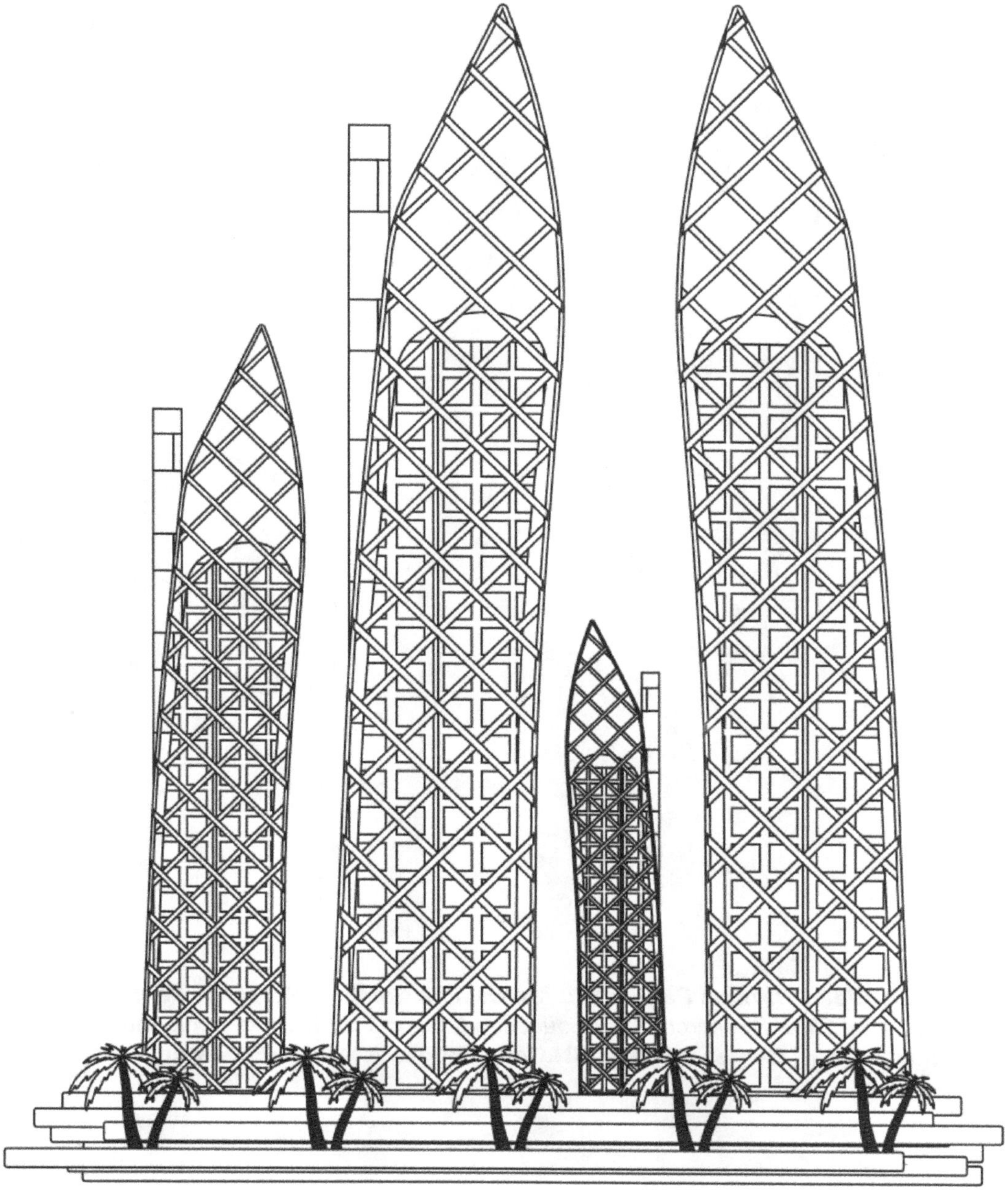

This is a Bleed Through Page If You Are Using a Coloring Marker or Pen!
Find Other Great Titles By searching for Educando Kids on Your Favorite Book Retailer
Amazon.Com | Barnes & Noble (BN.Com) | Books A Million (BAM.Com)

EDUCANDO KIDS

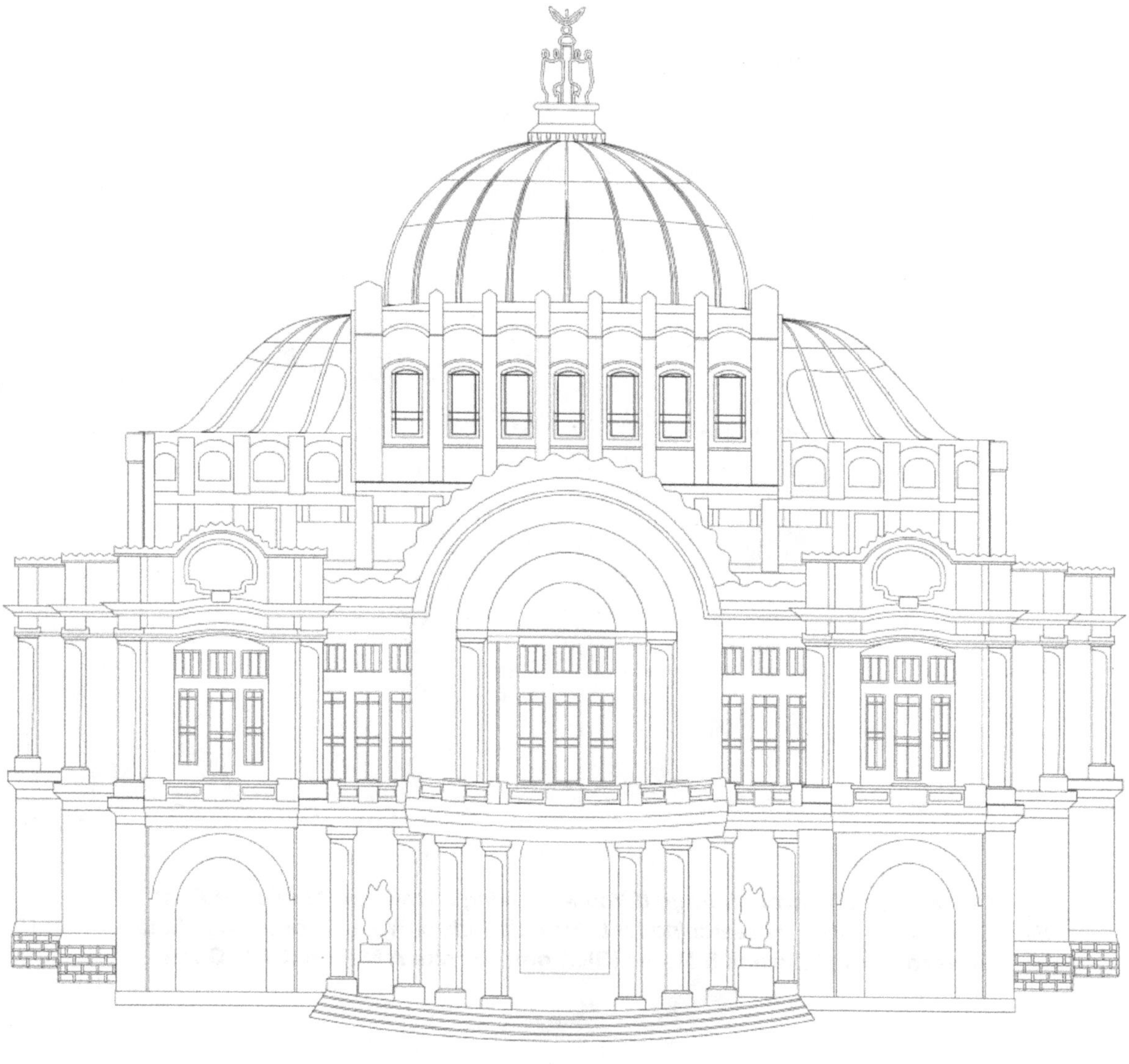

This is a Bleed Through Page If You Are Using a Coloring Marker or Pen!
Find Other Great Titles By searching for Educando Kids on Your Favorite Book Retailer
Amazon.Com | Barnes & Noble (BN.Com) | Books A Million (BAM.Com)

EDUCANDO KIDS

This is a Bleed Through Page If You Are Using a Coloring Marker or Pen!

Find Other Great Titles By searching for Educando Kids on Your Favorite Book Retailer

Amazon.Com | Barnes & Noble (BN.Com) | Books A Million (BAM.Com)

EDUCANDO KIDS

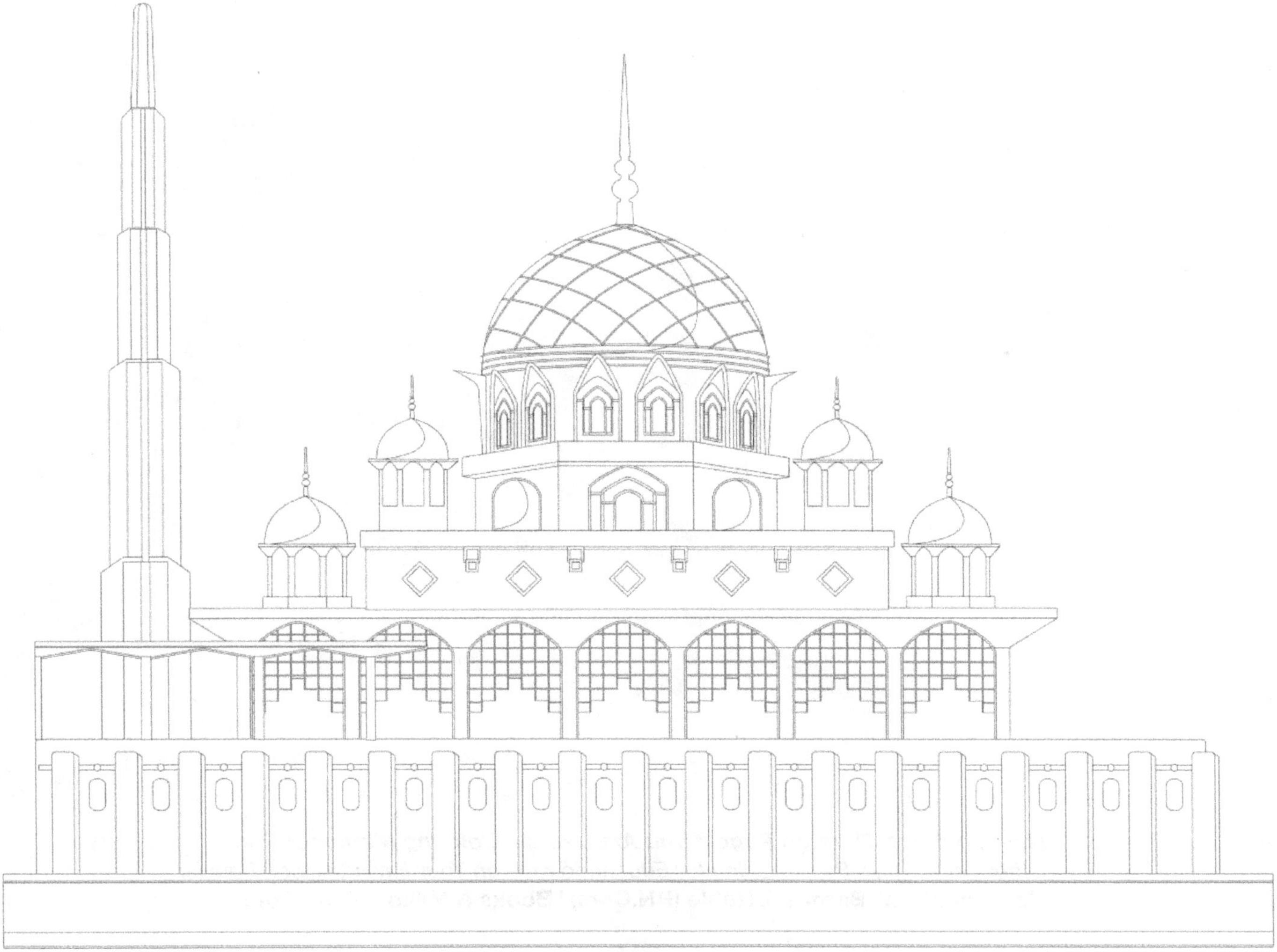

This is a Bleed Through Page If You Are Using a Coloring Marker or Pen!

Find Other Great Titles By searching for Educando Kids on Your Favorite Book Retailer

Amazon.Com | Barnes & Noble (BN.Com) | Books A Million (BAM.Com)

EDUCANDO KIDS

Printed in the USA
CPSIA information can be obtained
at www.ICGtesting.com
LVHW081136281123
765115LV00070B/2267

9 781645 211273